T0269793

BUTTERFLIES

Reflections, Tales, and Verse

BUTTERFLIES

HERMANN HESSE

Selected by Volker Michels
Illustrations by Jakob Hübner
Translated by Elisabeth Lauffer

KALES
PRESS

Kenneth Kales, Editor
Bonnie Thompson, Associate Editor
Sarah Bowen, Assistant Editor
Cover design by Laura Klynstra
Book design by Leah Carlson-Stanisic

Library of Congress Cataloging-in-Publication Data

Names: Hesse, Hermann, 1877–1962, author. | Michels, Volker, editor. |
Hübner, Jacob, 1761–1826 illustrator. | Lauffer, Elisabeth, translator
Title: Butterflies : reflections, tales, and verse / by Hermann Hesse ;
selected by Volker Michels ; illustrations by Jakob Hübner ; translated by Elisabeth Lauffer
Other titles: Schmetterlinge. English
Description: First edition | San Diego, California : Kales Press, [2023] |
Includes bibliographical references. | Summary: "An elegant collection
of Hermann Hesse's essays, passages, and poems on the subject of
butterflies and nature, accompanied by full-color copper-engraved
illustrations by Jakob Hübner"-- Provided by publisher.
Identifiers: LCCN 2022056416 (print) | LCCN 2022056417 (ebook)
| ISBN 9798985955859 (hardback) | ISBN 9798985955835 (ebook)
Subjects: LCSH: Butterflies.
Classification: LCC PT2617.E85 S3613 2023 (print) | LCC PT2617.E85
(ebook) | DDC 838/.91209--dc23/eng/20230207
LC record available at https://lccn.loc.gov/2022056416
LC ebook record available at https://lccn.loc.gov/2022056417

First Edition

Printed in Canada

ISBN-13: 979-8-9859558-5-9 print edition
ISBN-13: 979-8-9859558-3-5 e-book edition

kalespress.com
San Diego, California

CONTENTS

ON BUTTERFLIES

Everything we see is expression, all of nature an image, a language and vibrant hieroglyphic script. Despite our advanced natural sciences, we are neither prepared nor trained to really look at things, being rather at loggerheads with nature. Other eras, indeed, perhaps all other eras, all earlier periods before the earth fell to technology and industry, were attuned to nature's symbolic sorcery, reading its signs with greater simplicity, greater innocence than is our wont. This was by no means sentimental; the sentimental relationship people have with the natural world is a more recent development that may well arise from our troubled conscience with regard to that world.

A sense of nature's language, a sense of joy in the diversity displayed at every turn by life that begets life, and the drive to divine this varied language—or, rather, the drive to find answers—are as old as humankind itself. The wonderful instinct drawing us back to the dawn of time and the secret of our beginnings, instinct born of a sense of a concealed, sacred unity behind this extraordinary diversity, of a primeval mother behind all births, a creator behind all creatures, is the root of art, and always has been. Today it would seem we balk at revering nature in the pious sense of seeking oneness in manyness; we are reluctant to acknowledge this childlike drive and make jokes whenever reminded of it, yet we are likely wrong to think ourselves and contemporary humankind irreverent and incapable of piety in experiencing nature. It is just so difficult these days—really, it's become impossible—to do what was done in the past, innocently recasting nature as some mythical force or personifying and worshipping the Creator as a father. We may also be right in occasionally deeming old forms of piety somewhat silly or shallow, believing instead that the formidable, fateful drift toward philosophy we see happening in modern physics is ultimately a pious process.

So, whether we are pious and humble in our approach or pert and haughty, whether we mock or admire earlier expressions of belief in nature as animate: our actual relationship with nature, even when regarding it as a thing to be exploited, nevertheless remains that of a child with his mother, and the few age-old paths leading humans toward beatitude or wisdom have not grown in number. The simplest and most childlike of these paths is that of marveling at nature and warily heeding its language.

"I am here, that I may wonder!" reads a line by Goethe.

Wonder is where it starts, and though wonder is also where it ends, this is no futile path. Whether admiring a patch of moss, a crystal, flower, or golden beetle, a sky full of clouds, a sea with the serene, vast sigh of its swells, or a butterfly wing with its arrangement of crystalline ribs, contours, and the vibrant bezel of its edges, the diverse scripts and ornamentations of its markings, and the infinite, sweet, delightfully inspired transitions and shadings of its colors—whenever I experience part of nature, whether with my eyes or another of the five senses, whenever I feel drawn in, enchanted, opening myself momentarily to its existence and epiphanies, that very moment allows me to forget the avaricious, blind world of human need, and rather than thinking or issuing orders, rather than acquiring or exploiting, fighting or organizing, all I do in that moment is "wonder," like Goethe, and not only does this wonderment establish my brotherhood with him, other poets, and sages, it also makes me a brother to those wondrous things I behold and experience as the living world: butterflies and moths, beetles, clouds, rivers and mountains, because while wandering down the path of wonder, I briefly escape the world of separation and enter the world of unity, where one thing or creature says to the other: *Tat tvam asi* ("That thou art").

We look at the simpler relationship earlier generations had with nature and feel nostalgic now and then, or even envious, yet we prove unwilling to take our own times more seriously than warranted; nor do we wish to complain that our universities fail to guide us down the easiest paths to wisdom and that, rather than teaching a sense of awe, they teach the very opposite: counting and measuring over delight, sobriety over enchantment, a rigid hold on scattered individual parts over an affinity for the unified and whole. These are not schools of wisdom, after all, but schools of knowledge, though they take for granted that which they cannot teach—the capacity for experience, the capacity for being moved, the Goethean sense of wonderment—and keep mum about it, while their greatest minds recognize no nobler goal than to constitute a step toward such figures as Goethe and other true sages once more.

Butterflies, our intended focus here, are a beloved bit of creation, like flowers, favored by many as a prized and powerful object of astonishment, an especially lovely means of experience, of intuiting the great miracle, of honoring life. Like flowers, they seem specifically intended as adornment, jewelry or gems, little sparkling artworks and paeans invented by the friendliest, most charming and amusing of geniuses, dreamed up with tender creative delight. One must be blind or terribly callous not to delight at the sight of a butterfly, not to sense a remnant of childhood rapture or glimmer of Goethean wonder. And with good reason. After all, a butterfly is something special, an insect not like any other, and not really an insect at all, but the final, greatest, most festive and vitally important stage of its existence. As driven to procreate as it is prepared to die, it is the exuberant nuptial form of a creature that was until recently a slumbering pupa and, before that, a voracious caterpillar. A butterfly does not live to eat and grow old; its sole purpose is to make love and multiply. To that end, it is clad in magnificent finery. Its wings, several times larger than the body, divulge the secret of its existence in contours and color, scales and fuzz, a language both refined and varied, all in order that it may live out this existence with greater intensity, put on a more magical and tempting display for the opposite sex and glory in the celebration of procreation. People across the ages have known the significance of butterflies and their splendor; the butterfly is simply a revelation. Furthermore, because the butterfly is a festive lover and stunning shape-shifter, it has come to symbolize both impermanence and eternal persistence; from time immemorial, humans have embraced the butterfly as an allegorical and heraldic figure of the soul.

As it happens, the German term for butterfly, *Schmetterling*, is not very old; nor did all dialects use it. This peculiar word, while energetic in character, also feels quite raw, unsuitable even. Known and used only in Saxony and perhaps Thuringia, it did not enter the written language or general usage until the eighteenth century. *Schmetterling* was previously unknown in southern Germany and Switzerland, where the oldest and most beautiful word for butterflies was *Fifalter* (or *Zwiespalter**), but because human language, like the language and script found on butterfly wings, is a matter not of reason and calculation, but of creative and poetic potential, a single name did not suffice and, as is the case with everything we love, language instead produced several names—many, in fact. In Switzerland today, butterflies and moths are usually referred to as *Fifalter* or *Vogel* ("bird"), with such variations as *Tagvogel* ("day bird"), *Nacht-vogel* ("night bird"), and *Sommervogel* ("summer bird"). Given

---

* The use of the word *Zwiespalter* for butterflies is in reference to the bipartite quality of their bodies.—Translator.

the multitude of names for these creatures as a whole (including *Butterfliegen*, or "butter flies," *Molkendiebe*, or "whey thieves," and a range of others), which also change according to a region's landscape and dialect, one can imagine how many names must exist for individual butterfly species—though this will soon read "must have existed," for they are slowly dying out, like the names of local flowers, and if not for the children who discover a love of butterflies and collecting, these monikers, many of them marvelous, would gradually vanish as well, just as many areas have seen the wealth of butterfly species die out and disappear since industrialization and the rationalization of agriculture.

And on behalf of butterfly collectors, young and elderly alike, a further point bears mentioning. The fact that collectors kill butterflies and moths, stick them on pins, and preserve them, that they may endure and retain as much of their beauty as possible, for as long as possible, has been deemed—often with an air of sentimentality—an act of rank barbarism since the age of J.-J. Rousseau, and literature written between 1750 and 1850 features the comical figure of the pedant unable to enjoy or admire butterflies unless they are dead and skewered on pins. What was mostly nonsense, even then, is almost total nonsense today. There are, of course, collectors of all ages who

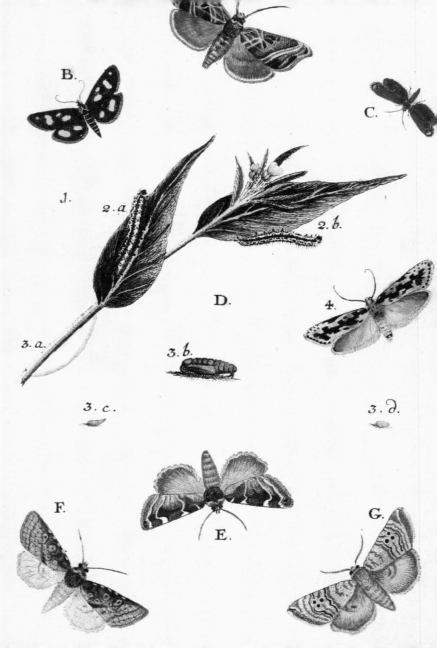

B.

C.

1.

2.a.

2.b.

D.

4.

3.a.

3.b.

3.c.

3.∂.

F.

E.

G.

will never content themselves with letting the creatures live and observing them in the wild, but even the roughest of this lot help ensure that butterflies aren't forgotten, that certain wonderful old names endure, and, at times, they contribute to our dear butterflies' very survival. Just as a love of hunting teaches nothing less than to tend one's prey, butterfly hunters were the first to recognize how the eradication of certain plants (e.g., stinging nettles) and other acts of violence in an ecosystem can lead to the rapid dwindling of butterfly populations. Not that the cabbage white or a similar foe of the farmer and gardener would suffer any losses; instead, it's the finer, rarer, and prettier species losing the battle and disappearing whenever humans get too involved in a landscape. A true butterfly lover does more than treat the caterpillar, pupa, and eggs with care; he also does what he can to allow for as many types of butterflies as possible to flourish in his area. I myself, though many years have passed since my days as a collector, have been known to sow nettles.

Every child with a butterfly collection has heard of the much bigger, much brighter, much more brilliant butterflies found in hotter climes, in India, Brazil, or Madagascar. Some have even laid eyes on them, in museums or personal collections, because these days one can purchase exotic butterflies, preserved (often beautifully so) and mounted on cotton under glass; even those who haven't glimpsed them have seen reproductions. When I was younger, I remember, I very badly wanted to see one particular butterfly that my books told me could be found in Andalusia in the month of May. And whenever I encountered some magnificent specimen of the tropics in a museum or a friend's collection, I felt that indescribable delight of childhood tugging at me, something akin to the thrill I had, for instance, experienced as a boy the first time I spotted an Apollo. Accompanying this delight, which contains its share of melancholy, at the sight of such wondrous creatures I would often take that step out of my not-always-so-poetic life and into Goethean wonder, experiencing a moment of enchantment, devotion, and piety.

And later, what I never thought possible happened to me, as I myself sailed the seas to disembark on sultry foreign coasts. I traveled by crocodile-infested waters through tropical forests to see tropical butterflies in their natural habitat. With that, many of my boyhood dreams came true, and in coming true, some also tarnished. The fascination with butterflies, however, never flagged; this little door to the ineffable, this lovely and effortless pathway to awe, has rarely quit me.

The first time I saw tropical butterflies in flight was in Penang;

the first time I caught one was in Kuala Lumpur; and for a splendid, brief spell I lived on the Batang Hari River in Sumatra, where by night I heard wild thunderstorms ravaging the jungle and by day I watched unfamiliar butterflies floating in forest clearings, with their fantastic greens and golds, their gem tones. None of them, when later seen preserved on needles or under glass, was quite as thrilling or magical as they had been outside, among roving shadows and light, where they were still alive, where the colors of their wings were animated from within, where the color was joined by movement—that oft-expressive, enigmatic flight—and where the miracle was not surrendered so dully to my curiosity, but had to be espied and experienced in the moment, as by a hunter. Nevertheless, it is astonishing how well butterflies keep. Most colorful creatures, fauna and flora alike, lose what makes them most beautiful after death, however expertly preserved. Should flowers not serve as sufficient example, one need only consider the plumage of a bird just shot by the hunter, then consider the same bird half a day later: its blue, yellow, green, or red remains, but a hostile tinge has encroached. There's something missing: it still shimmers but no longer shines, something is extinguished and gone, never to return. The difference is much less pronounced among butterflies, moths, and some beetles, whose splendor, even in death, is far better maintained than other creatures'. They will last a very long time, decades even, provided they're stored away from pests and sunlight.

The Malayan people, whose lands I once toured, had their own names for butterflies, various names, all beautiful. The sound of their collective term for "butterfly" contained a living memory of the dichotomous winged creature, just as it's echoed in the old German words *Zwiespalter* and *Fifalter* or the Italian *farfalla*, and so on. Malays typically called butterflies either *kupu kupu* or *lapa lapa*, after the sound of fluttering. There is as much vital beauty, expressiveness, and unconscious creative power in this *lapa lapa* as in the peacock butterfly's eyespots or the letter *C* limned in white on the sooty underside of some native species' wings.

Whosoever studies the images of these fairy-tale beings, may they be overcome—here, there, and everywhere—by the great sense of wonder that precedes recognition and reverence.

A BUTTERFLY

Visited by utter woe,
Roaming the fields I did espy
Upon my way a butterfly
Clad in white and darkling red,
All aflutter in the blow.

Oh, you! And I, a child,
The world still so very clear,
And skies still so very near,
That day I last saw you part
Those lovely wings so wide.

Flutter of color against blue skies,
From paradise itself you came,
While I, alien and full of shame,

Beheld your godly splendor
With dim and useless eyes!

Off across the fields it flew,
That white-and-scarlet butterfly.
And as I dreamily wandered by,
What lingered on of paradise
Was splendor, still and true.

MY EARLIEST MEMORY

✧

The furthest I can trace back memories of constancy and early experiences is age five. What I encounter first is an image of my surroundings, my parents and our house as well as the city and region in which I was raised. Our open, sunny street, with its single row of buildings just outside the city, made an impression at the time, as did the burg's more imposing features—city hall, cathedral, and bridges spanning the Rhine—and, most importantly, the meadowlands behind our house, which extended without limit for my little legs. I was more captivated by the innumerable particulars found in that landscape than I was aware of my own feelings or the people around me, even of portraits of my parents. My memory of the meadow seems older than any remembrance of human faces or personal mishaps. A diffidence, accompanied from a young age by revulsion when unfamiliar hands—whether those of a doctor or a domestic—touched my body without permission, may explain the pleasure I found in being outdoors by myself. I would walk for hours, my destination the untrodden green wilds found in that great meadow. Recalling those periods of solitude fills me with the same pained happiness that largely characterizes the paths of childhood. The scent of grass from that plain still wafts about me in delicate clouds, along with the peculiar conviction that no other time and no other place could produce such wonderful quaking grasses and butterflies, such lush water plants, such golden buttercups or glorious campions, primroses, bellflowers, and scabiosas. I never have encountered such perfectly slender plantago, such bright yellow stonecrop, such enticing, iridescent lizards and butterflies, and my mind is reluctant to linger on the realization that it isn't the flowers and lizards that have changed for the worse but, rather, my own spirit and eye.

At the thought of the meadow, I cannot help but conclude that whatever I later came to behold or possess, however precious, including my art, was meager in comparison to that landscape's grandeur. Some bright mornings I would lie there, head on my hands, and gaze over a crinkled sea of grasses shimmering in the sunlight, dotted with islands of red poppies, blue bellflowers, and purple bittercress. I was tantalized by electric-yellow brimstones and delicate common blues fluttering overhead; by purple emperors and painted ladies bathed in a sumptuous shimmer, almost antiquarian in its rarity; by the mourning cloak's heavy wings, by game-like Old World and scarce swallowtails, black-winged red admirals, and the singular Apollo, its name reflective of the veneration it inspires. The latter, which I recognized from friends' descriptions, flew toward me one day and alighted on the ground, where it slowly fanned its marvelous alabaster wings, allowing me to see the fine markings and contours, stark diamantine lines, and pairs of bloodred eyespots. Little from this distant past has remained as fresh in my memory as the breathless, heart-pounding elation at that sight. Given the capriciousness innate to children, however, I stalked the fine creature and threw my hat at it. It looked around, rose with an elegant swoop, and vanished forthwith in the radiant sunlight.

My approach to catching and collecting butterflies was never scientific in the least. I wasn't remotely concerned with the caterpillars or the names of butterflies, known in those parts as *Sommervöglein* or *Sommervögli* ("little summer birds"), and in many cases, I invented my own monikers. There were the reddish flies I called *Zitterlinge* ("shudderflies") and a species of brown *Schnabler* ("beakies"). I scornfully referred to the ragtag crew of white, Scotch argus, and other common, plain butterflies as "dunderheads." I did not treat my plunder with care and never managed to assemble a tidy collection.

BLUE BUTTERFLY

Blue little butterfly
Blown here on the wind,
Pearly shiver in the sky
Glitters, flutters, meets its end.

In the twinkling of an eye,
Borne past me by that wind,
I watched happiness wave goodbye,
Glittering, fluttering, meeting its end.

THE GIANT PEACOCK MOTH

卂

My friend Heinrich Mohr, who was visiting at the time, had returned from an evening stroll and joined me in my study as daylight faded. The distant lake was visible from the windows, pale waters bounded starkly by a hilly shoreline. My little boy had just said good night, so our conversation turned to children and childhood memories.

"Having children," I mused, "has revived certain pastimes from my own youth. For the last year or so, I've been collecting butterflies again. Care to see?"

He agreed, and I went to retrieve two or three of the light-weight cardboard cases. As I opened the first, we were struck by how dark it was in the room; one could barely discern the outline of the pinned specimens.

I reached for the lamp and struck a match, and presently the outside scenery withdrew, the windows now an impenetrable midnight blue.

In the bright lamplight, however, my butterflies gleamed magnificently. Leaning over the case, we studied the colorful shapes and recited their names.

"This is a yellow bands underwing," I said. "*Fulminea* in Latin. Rare in these parts."

Holding it by the pin, Heinrich had carefully removed one of the butterflies from the case and was inspecting it from below.

"Strange," he said. "Nothing brings back my childhood like the sight of butterflies."

Then, pinning the creature back in place and closing the lid, he said, "Enough!"

His manner was brusque, as though these were unwelcome memories. Once I returned from stowing away the cases, a smile appeared on his narrow, tanned face and he asked for a cigarette.

"Don't hold it against me," he said, "for not studying your collection more closely. I had one as a boy too, of course, but unfortunately I spoiled the very memory of it. I can tell you the story, though it's really quite shameful."

He leaned over the oil lamp to light his cigarette, replaced the green lampshade, which pitched our faces into darkness, then sat on the sill by the open window, his gaunt form scarcely perceptible in the shadows. And as I smoked my cigarette and the faraway song of frogs filled the night, my friend told me the following:

"I started collecting butterflies when I was eight or nine. I wasn't particularly zealous at first, and pursued it as I would any other game or hobby, but by the second summer, maybe around age ten, I was hooked. In its thrall, I would forget or neglect everything around me, to the point where the adults in my life thought they might have to forbid it. While out chasing butterflies, I was deaf to the clock tower sounding the start of school or lunchtime, and during vacations I'd often set out in the early morning and not return till night, not come home for a single meal, with just a bit of bread packed in my botanical field box.

"Even now, a hint of that passion will return at the sight of a beautiful butterfly. For a few moments, I'm overcome by the nameless, hungry delight that only children feel, and that I felt as a boy the first time I stalked a swallowtail. Countless moments and hours of childhood then come flooding back, blazing afternoons in the parched, fragrant heath, cool mornings in the garden or evenings along the shadowy edges of the forest, where I stood on the lookout, net in hand, like a treasure hunter ready at any moment for the most wondrous surprises and delights to appear. Whether the butterfly was rare or not, whenever I saw a pretty one perched on a flower stem in the sun, opening and closing its vibrant wings with each breath, the desire to hunt took my own breath away, and as I crept in closer and closer, till I could see every gleaming color and every crystalline vein and every fine brown hair on its feelers—there was a sense of tension and rapture, a mix of tender joy and wild desire that I have seldom felt since.

"I had to store my collection in a regular old cardboard box, as my parents were poor and unable to give me anything else. I stuck the pins into little cork disks I had sliced from bottle stoppers and glued in place along the bottom of the dented box, where I tended my treasures. I readily shared my collection with my schoolmates at first, but they all had wooden cases with glass lids, caterpillar kits with green mesh walls, and other luxuries, leaving me little to boast about, what with my primitive setup. I didn't have much need to brag, anyway, and got used to keeping mum about my catches, even major ones, which I only showed my sisters. I did, however, once capture and prepare a rare purple emperor, and as soon as it dried, pride compelled me to show my neighbor, the son of a teacher who lived across the way. This boy had the vice of flawlessness, a trait doubly unsettling in children. Though trifling, his own

collection was a gem, it was so neat, so fastidiously maintained. He had even mastered the singular and vexatious art of gluing back together damaged butterfly wings and was a model child in every respect, which made me despise him out of equal parts envy and admiration.

"I presented my purple emperor to the Perfect Boy. He expertly examined the specimen, acknowledged its rarity, and appraised its cash value at about twenty pfennigs, as young Emil was practiced in valuating all manner of collectibles, especially postage stamps and butterflies. But then he began to criticize my find, said the purple emperor was poorly mounted, its right feeler bent, the left extended, and discovered yet another real defect, namely that the butterfly was missing two legs. I wasn't terribly bothered by these issues, but that stickler had dampened my joy, and I never shared with him again.

"Two years later, though by then we were grown boys, my passion was still in full bloom when I heard a rumor that Emil had bagged a giant peacock moth. The news was more exhilarating than if I were to learn today that a friend had inherited millions or unearthed the lost books of Livy. None of us had ever caught a giant peacock moth. The closest I had ever come to seeing one was an illustration in an old butterfly book, whose hand-colored copperplate etchings were far more lovely and, indeed, far more precise than any modern color prints. Of all the butterflies and moths I could name that were missing from my box, there were none I coveted as desperately. I had studied the image many times. A friend once told me that when birds or other predators attack one of these brown moths as it rests on a branch or rock, it simply unfolds its dark forewings to display handsome hind wings with big, bright eyespots so unexpected that the bird flies off in surprise, leaving the moth in peace.

"And now that dullard Emil had one of these wondrous creatures! When I first heard the news, I was ecstatic, ablaze with curiosity at the prospect of seeing the rare moth, at long last. Then, of course, envy set in. It seemed outrageous to me that, of all people, that pudgy old bore had managed to nab this precious, enigmatic moth. So I restrained myself and stayed put, thus denying him the pleasure of showing off his catch. I couldn't stop thinking about it, though, and when the rumor was confirmed at school the next day, I decided to pay him a visit after all.

"The moment we finished eating and I was excused from the table, I dashed across the courtyard and up to the fourth floor of our neighbors' house, where—tucked between unfinished chambers and the maid's quarters—the teacher's son had an enviable little den all to himself. I didn't encounter anyone on the way upstairs, and there was no response when I knocked on his door. Emil wasn't there, but when I tried the handle, the door opened, though he was usually careful to lock up. I wanted to see the creature, at the very least, so in I went and immediately spotted the two big boxes Emil used for his collection. I checked both in vain, then realized the moth would still be on the spreading board. And that's where I found it. The giant peacock moth hung on the board, its brown wings spanned with thin strips of paper, and I leaned in to study it up close: its hairy, tan feelers, the elegant and inexpressibly delicate coloring of the wings' edges, the fine fuzz along the inside of the hind wings. The eyespots were the only part I couldn't see; they were covered by the paper.

"I gave in to temptation, my heart pounding as I removed the paper and pulled out the pin. Four big, strange eyes gazed up at me, far more beautiful and bizarre than in the diagrams I'd seen. The sight filled me with the desire to possess the magnificent creature, a desire so overpowering that, without a second thought, I committed the first theft of my life, scuttling out, the moth—which had already dried and thus held its form—gently cupped in my hand. All I felt in that moment was immense satisfaction.

"With the creature concealed in my right hand, I headed downstairs. I heard someone approaching from below, and in that moment my conscience awakened and I realized that I'd stolen, that I was a louse. At the same time, I was seized by a terrible fear of being discovered, so I instinctively stuck my hand, still holding the plunder, into my jacket pocket. I was trembling as I slowly continued, gripped by a cold feeling of depravity and shame, and passed fearfully by the maid as she climbed the stairs, then paused at the front door, my heart racing and brow damp, stunned and horrified by my own actions.

"I knew at once that the moth was not mine to keep, that I must return it and undo what I had done. And so, despite my fear of exposure, I wheeled about, leapt up the stairs, and a minute later found myself back in Emil's room. I gingerly withdrew my hand from my pocket and placed the moth on the table. The moment I saw it, I knew the damage was done. I could have wept, for the moth was destroyed. The right forewing and feeler were missing, and though I sought carefully to remove the detached wing from my pocket, it was ravaged, the very thought of repair impossible.

"The sight of the exquisite, rare creature I had mutilated was almost more devastating than the feeling of having stolen. My fingers were dusted with its fine brown scales, and seeing the torn wing lying there, I would have given anything, any possession, any pleasure, to have it restored.

"I went home sad that afternoon and sat in our little garden until dusk, when I worked up the courage to tell my mother what had happened. Though I sensed her dismay, she could also see that this confession had cost me more than any punishment might.

"'You have to go tell Emil,' she said decisively. 'That's the one thing you can do, and until that happens, I cannot forgive you. You can offer him something of yours in return, and you have to ask for his forgiveness.'

"Had it been anyone but him, the Perfect Boy, this wouldn't have felt so daunting. I could already see that he wouldn't understand and might not even believe me, and as evening gave way to night, I still hadn't gone. My mother found me in the front hallway and said quietly, 'It has to happen today. Off you go.'

"I went over and asked for Emil. He came and immediately told me someone had ruined his giant peacock moth, though he didn't know if it was some rascal who'd done it, or maybe a bird or the cat, and I asked him to take me upstairs and show me. We went up, he unlocked the door and lit a candle, and I saw the mangled form on the spreading board. I could tell he had tried to mend it; the broken wing was carefully arranged on a piece of damp blotting paper, but it was irreparable, and anyhow, one of its feelers was missing.

"Then I told him it was me, and tried to explain what had happened.

"Rather than blow up and start screaming, Emil whistled gently through his teeth, studied me in silence, then said, 'So, you're one of those.'

"I offered him all my toys. He remained cool, though, his gaze scornful, so I offered my entire butterfly collection, to which he responded, 'Thanks, but I've seen your collection, and besides, today you showed us yet again how you treat butterflies.'

"It wouldn't have taken much in that moment for me to throttle him. There was no helping the situation. I was nothing but a scoundrel, while Emil stood before me like the world order, a vision of restrained, contemptuous righteousness. He didn't even tell me off; he just looked at me in disgust.

"That was when I realized you cannot make amends for what's already ruined. I returned home, relieved when my mother didn't ask any questions, but simply gave me a kiss and left me alone. I should have gone to bed, as it was already late, but before I did, I stole into the dining room, retrieved the big brown box, set it on my bed, and opened it in the dark. Then I took out the butterflies, one by one, and ground them to dust and tatters between my fingers."

DEDICATION TO A POETRY COLLECTION

Leaves drifting from the tree,
Songs of life's reverie
Lift nimbly on the breeze;
Much here has passed
Since we sang them last,
Those gentle melodies.

Songs, too, in time will fade,
For to endure they are not made,
The wind, it scatters and it scours:
Symbols themselves temporal
Of all things immortal,
Butterflies and flowers.

The traveler lay alone, just off the path, in the warm sun. His eyes followed the play of light on the yellow cliffs; his ears were soothed by the sound of a mountain stream behind him, which barely reached him from the distance, low and steady. Somewhere between wakefulness and sleep, his soul hung like a bird on the wing over the bright landscape of his childhood. A brown butterfly sailed slowly past the roadside wall, its haphazard course cleaving through the narrow outline of the lake, which shone in the man's eyes where he lay. Against the dark green, gleaming ground, the butterfly's matte hues looked richer and brighter. The delicate edges of its wings trembled in a white sunbeam, as though this distinct, motile shape were attracting the light.

The fervent delights of childhood rose in the resting man's memory: the ecstasy of chasing butterflies in summer, the hunt among garden beds' great blossoms and in fragrant, hushed meadows, where the hot air shimmered in luminous waves.

The dreamer's eyelids grew heavy and closed unnoticed. His dream ran breathlessly across the meadows and hillsides of home, chasing butterflies, and from the unveiled depths of distant memory, a long-forgotten childhood yearning swept over the sleeper: to glimpse a mountain Apollo. The object of eager young desires, snow-white with red markings, the beautiful king of butterflies appeared to hang above him in the blue. Other strangely sweet melodies returned, familiar and gentle, from years past. The serene skies of youth bowed brilliantly in avid blueness over the traveler's slumberous thoughts.

A cool breeze came in from the mountains opposite and grazed the sleeper's lowered brow. He smiled and slowly opened his eyes, refreshed by the clean lake air and the cheery colors of the landscape, and rose with pleasure.

Then a white flash glided past. He paused and looked up, listening. Inaudible and unhurried, a pale butterfly descended in an elegant arc, flew along the ground, fluttered, eyes surveying, then settled on the surface of a sloping, sun-burnished boulder. It appeared to be listening as well, moving its fine antennae; then it quietly spread all four wings in the warm light. Apollo! Delicate dark veins with a metallic glint ran through the silken white wings, and against this pale background, magnificent carmine eyespots emerged.

The mountain Apollo closed its wings, accentuating their fine, long form and flawless curves, then stretched out once more, as though drawing breath, turned, and took off. It flew from the rock to the tip of a tall violet thistle, and from there toward the lake, into the dark depths. Then it rose again, hovered indecisively for a moment, beat its wings in rapture several times, and disappeared upward into the vast glowing skies.

BUTTERFLY IN WINE

A butterfly flew into my glass of wine,
Drunk and resigned to its sweet goodbye,
Flagging, it paddles, willing to die;
Until finally my finger averts its decline.

Blinded by your eyes, such is my heart,
Blissfully deep in the redolent glass,
Drunk on your magic, willing to pass,
Unless a wave of your hand puts an end to my part.

THE YELLOW TIGER MOTH

⚜

Lunchtime chatter in Preda was dominated by the Alpine tiger.

"I've been stalking tigers for five days and haven't caught a single one!"

"I already bagged two. One's a female."

"I spotted one yesterday, but there was no catching it."

One of the gentlemen turned to me. "Have you come across any?"

"Alpine tigers?"

"Well, yes."

I paused for a moment to think. I was more than a little ashamed not to have known that tigers lived in this part of Graubünden. I opted for denial over betraying my ignorance.

"Haven't seen one yet," I responded nonchalantly, "but I've heard them roar a few times."

The man's eyes widened. He gaped at me, shook his head, and burst into laughter.

"I take it you're not an entomologist?" he asked, still chuckling.

"No, what's that?"

"Another name for butterfly collector. The yellow 'tiger,' *Arctia flavia*, is an Alpine moth species native to this region. We're all after it."

"Is that so? I always thought catching butterflies was for children."

"Not at all! But, if I may ask—if you aren't an entomologist, what brings you to Preda?"

The question struck me as naïve, considering Preda's beauty and situation high in the Albula Alps, three hours from the top of the pass. Every last mountain in the area demands to be climbed, Piz Val Lunga and nearby Piz Moulix* in particular. Within a few days, however, the horrid fellow proved to be right. The town is scarcely more than a small station and two inns, both of which are overrun with entomologists. Butterfly nets, vials of ether, and carbide lamps litter the place. Nets flutter in every meadow and on every scree field; serious men

* The Romansh names Piz Moulix, and Piz Loleis to come on page 49, denote mountain peaks in the Swiss canton of Graubünden, where the Rhaeto-Romanic language is predominantly spoken.—Translator.

can be found turning over rock after rock, checking for A. *fla-via* eggs. There are collectors who have been coming here for at least five summers running, some of whom have plundered thirty or more of these rare Alpine specimens, while others look nervous and resigned after having hunted certain butter-flies in vain for years.

There are those among them, no doubt, who would prove pleasant in everyday life, but here on the playground of their pas-sions, they become fanatical and impossible. Each slavers for prey, each keeps a close eye on the others. After making a rare catch, a fellow will fib about where he found it, unaware that at least one of his comrades was trailing him and noted the site. Every last one has spots or experiences he will take to the grave. And should a dreaded rival topple over a wall and break his bones, the others receive the news with poorly feigned sympathy.

This all makes for rather an excruciating stay in Preda. Even worse is the threat of contagion. Indeed, it came to pass about eight days in, while on a frosty hike with my travel companion, that I declared my intention to start a butterfly collection when I got home, and that I'd use ether, rather than potassium cya-nide, to kill the creatures. My friend gave me a bemused look, and I became aware of the precarity of my condition. I resolved to leave at once. That evening, though, I found I still wanted a peek at what the entomologists were doing; I joined one of their tours and have no regrets. It was my finest night in Preda.

We left after dinner, two butterfly catchers, my friend, and I. It was still light out, and we slowly walked up the scenic road, past Lai da Palpuogna, a spectacular little Alpine lake with a big, dark blue eye at the center of its glassy green surface.

"Look at those marvelous black trees along the shore! It's like a fairy tale."

"Yes, those are larches, and there may be a few geometer moths flying about. Should we check?"

"Heavens, no."

"Onward, then. There's the Weissenstein."

The Weissenstein, once a popular inn, closed when the Albula Railway was built and now serves as the primary starting point for entomological raids. From there, it is just an hour to Flaviafelsen, the best-known hunting grounds for the yellow tiger.

A comfortable footpath branches to the left off the Albula Pass, leading past a waterfall and several large, barren scree fields toward the inn. We climbed slowly, rolling over all the big rocks along the way, some as tall as people, in the hopes of uncovering moth eggs or pupae. All we found, though, was a single empty cocoon. We got lost as we moved uphill, and had to exercise great caution in steep areas, so as not to strike one another as we turned the blocks of stone. This rather wearisome task was made more appealing when a herdsman told us there were scores of vipers beneath the loose rocks, but we caught no glimpse of the snakes, either; everything seemed dead, the desolation punctuated intermittently by the shrill, almost scornful whistle of a distant marmot.

Our fruitless efforts vexed me, and as darkness fell, it became almost impossible to work in the detritus. Beyond the talus, I came upon a patch of meadow nearly free of stones, where I could make my way up the slope with ease. I left the other three behind for a spell and climbed the steep hillside into the gathering darkness, my ascent aimless, my thoughts few. Small rocks quietly tumbled away beneath my feet, and the tip of my alpenstock occasionally shrilled in the cracks, but beyond the gentle groan of my hobnailed boots, all was still.

In the meanwhile, the first stars had risen unseen above the opposite peak, and when I paused to rest and turned about, I beheld a stunning sight. The bare mountainside plunged deep into the Albula Valley, a brown wasteland. Countless tiny spring-fed lakes emitted a pale gleam amid moorlands and

116.

117.

118.

stony heaths, the reflection of stars swimming in each. Across the broad, magnificent high valley, the sharp contours of the twins—Piz Loleis and the Albulahorn—rose into the night sky. In the uncertain greenish starlight, everything appeared forsaken, wilder and bigger than during daytime. Barring the fluid silver glow of a foggy, windswept morning, I cannot imagine conditions better suited to casting this mountain pass in its natural grandiosity than the cold, gray-green, and gauzy light of a clear yet moonless night.

The sight of the entomologists hunting far below was half-ghostly, half-comical. The blinding light of their dark lanterns illuminated a white linen sheet they had spread out. I watched the hunters dance hastily—though carefully, on the stony slope—about the quietly flickering shaft of light, swinging their white butterfly nets in hurried arcs and circles, trying to catch the moths drawn to the glow. They became indistinct, frenzied blots when they moved out of the light, only to return suddenly to focus when they stepped back into the beam; from time to time, one would slip on the ground or kneel to gather up his catch. It was like a nocturnal dance of madmen. The scene was unforgettable: this Alpine valley, its expanse magnified in the night, bounded by immense mountains, with these two tiny, fervid humans indulging in a harmlessly wonderful desire.

Upon my return, I found one of the lanterns extinguished, its owner straining to contain his rage, while the other butter-fly catcher continued his pursuit quietly, a smile on his face. We persuaded him to wrap things up as well, then headed home by the light of his lantern. I inquired about the hunt; one of the collectors had gotten lucky and was pleased, whereas the man whose lantern had failed grumbled to himself.

"It would seem your friend fared a sight better?" I said to him.

"Yes," he growled. "Half-wits have all the luck."

The other man heard, but grinned to himself in satisfaction all the same, though he had not caught the yellow tiger, either. I alone was lucky enough to see one. When I turned on the light in my room after our late return, it flew against the window. I didn't trap it, though; nor did I tell the collectors. It was a pretty creature, black and yellowish brown, with a thick, hairy body. I gave the moth a nod, turned out the light, and watched it vanish, wings aflutter, into the blue night.

CONFESSION

See how soon, fair apparition,
I submit to your schemes;
While others have purpose or ambition,
Simply living will do for me.

Whatever once has touched my soul
Appears to me a metaphor
Of the infinite, of the whole,
That I felt, evermore.

Life will e'er reward my seeing
Deeper meaning in such sights,
For the Eternal, for pure Being,
I know within me do reside.

INDIAN BUTTERFLIES

※

Kandy is said to be the prettiest destination on the beautiful island of Ceylon, and the railway journey there from Colombo is a delightful succession of surprises and attractions. Kandy itself represents the remains of a very old royal and religious capital, and more recently, British money has managed to transform it into a tidy, comfortable, blighted den of tourists and hotels. Still, Kandy is beautiful, because all the money and all the cement in the world are no match for this landscape's lavish growth. One sees boisterous bushes and trees on verdant slopes choked out by yet more boisterous creepers, while daringly full-blossomed, fragrant morning glories and clematis bloom and cascade into the valley, where an artificial lake suffers from grotesquely inorganic features, an incurable complaint. Plucky Brits perambulate about this lake, where old women mow the grounds with rusty swords, and these English strollers do not feel harassed by the incessant crush of coachmen, rickshaw pullers, merchants, and beggars shamelessly offering themselves up; the English are rich, after all, ingenious colonizers whose primary source of pleasure is witnessing the demise of the populations they have overwhelmed, a demise, in their minds, that is nothing if not humane, pleasant, and peaceful: neither murder nor even exploitation but, rather, a quiet, mild corruption and moral annihilation. Nevertheless, the English have style, and were this a French or German enterprise, they would bungle it, just as the Englishman is the sole European whose presence among primitive peoples does not seem to be amiss. I was not to be deterred, either, and tried to see as much of Kandy as possible on my very first day. This is no mean feat for one with open ears and a rather delicate constitution, as a walk through the city amounts to running a strenuous, maddening gauntlet of tourist-industry hyenas; even in Europe, this experience can be found only at sites that have known the benefit of English lucre. By the end, one is only too happy to submit to the grinning rickshaw driver who obstructed one's path with the handles of his cart twenty times, and whom one chased off twenty times; he was right, he knew very well that he and his cohort would ensure that any newcomer's attempt to wander about Kandy ended in a taxi.

Still, one learns to live with most things. I had come to terms with the heat in Singapore and in Colombo, mosquitoes in the jungle, unfamiliar cuisine, diarrhea, and colic, so it must be possible here, too. I learned to look past sweet little girls as they begged forlornly. I learned to harden my gaze to repel white-haired great-grandfathers who looked like saints. I grew accustomed to a dedicated retinue of people whose services were available for purchase, a horde I kept in check by means of military-style hand gestures and gruff commands. I even learned to swallow the dreadful insight that most of these Indians' soulful, beseeching eyes were not calling for deities and redemption, but simply for money.

Just as I was reaching that point, in a fit of madness fueled by high spirits, I set out one afternoon with my butterfly net. I anticipated that this would provoke the street children's curiosity and maybe even ridicule—something I had learned to take in stride from the otherwise good-natured Malays—and sure enough, all the little ones laughed and hollered in Sinhalese. A student passed by with books under his arm, and I asked him what their barbs meant. He smiled politely and murmured, "Oh, sir, they are laughing that you are an Englishman who is trying to catch butterflies!" If the children's looks were any indication, however, their taunts had been considerably less innocuous. I continued happily on my way, and was not surprised when children joined who wanted to show me good butterfly spots, and who eagerly pointed out every fly that buzzed by, then held out their hands for a penny. This no longer fazed me, and as the street grew quieter and a narrow path into the woods appeared, promising solitude, I breathed a sigh of relief, mustered my final scrap of good humor, and sent the last of my chaperones running as I turned toward refuge.

Man will thus blindly go his way, fancying himself victorious when he has, in fact, been vanquished. I strutted along, congratulating myself for how very cleverly I had handled yet another situation, while my doom was already decided, a fishing line cast unnoticed, a hook I would long be swallowing. Hanging thirty paces behind me the entire time was a comely, quiet man or gentleman with wavy black hair, doleful dark eyes, and a fine black mustache. His name, I would learn, was Victor Hughes, and I was fated to fall victim to him.

He approached and greeted me deferentially, smiled most politely, and informed me in flawless English that this path led to a stone quarry and there was no hope of finding butterflies here. Over there, though, more to the right, wasn't bad, and across the valley to the south was one of the very best spots. Before I had said much more than Yes or No or Thank you, we had fallen into a conversation and made a personal connection of sorts; from behind this beautiful human's intelligent, concerned eyes, a noble, old, oppressed people gazed at me in reproachful silence, and his words and gestures communicated an ancient culture of cultivated manners and Buddhist serenity. I immediately came to love this man with a mixture of pity and esteem. Being a white stranger in a pith helmet made me the *sahib*, to whom he, the poor native, was expected to bow; his aristocratic air, however, coupled with his local knowledge, sweeping expertise, and superb English, immediately revealed his superiority to me. Victor Hughes, I soon learned, knew infinitely more about butterflies than I did; with a collegial smile, he recited scores of Latin names I had never heard, though I nodded condescendingly to mask my childish dilettantism. I interjected a few times, adopting the sheepishly paternal tone the English often employed when addressing natives: "Yes, yes, my dear man, I know all about Kandy's butterflies!" He spoke to me about Indian butterflies the way a veteran head groundsman in a palm garden might speak to a foreign tourist who fancies himself a botanist. My poor English, which I used as little as possible, prevented me from explaining myself, and without realizing it, I became entangled in a lie, though I had barely said a word. In my mute playacting, I stepped further and further into the role of an expert scientific collector.

After we had reached an understanding—after I had tacitly granted Mr. Hughes the right to view me as a slightly more distinguished colleague and to ascribe to me interests and intents that I frankly did not have—he surprised me by producing a pretty little wooden case from his robes, as if by magic. My immediate suspicions were confirmed when an obsequious peddler's smile appeared on his genteel face; he opened the box with an inviting gesture, and I saw a fetching, impeccably preserved collection of butterflies and beetles against a white background, which he offered me for the trifling sum of fifteen rupees.

I saw the scope of the danger at once, but had no defense. It was impossible for me to alter my stance so suddenly toward this polite, almost erudite Sinhalese. If anything, with his aims, his masked indigence thus revealed, my sympathy (or at least my pity) for him grew. Still, I did not want to buy anything, compelled as I was to exercise restraint with what remained of my travel funds.

I explained to him, with a new coolness to my tone, that although a collector, I did not purchase butterflies and, moreover, that ready-made specimens were of no interest to me.

Mr. Hughes understood entirely. But, of course, such collectors as I would never buy mounted butterflies; he had figured that and merely wanted to show me a small sample. Naturally I would limit my purchases to fresh specimens in paper bags, which he hoped to show me this evening. He knew I was staying at Queens Hotel: would I be available at six o'clock?

I didn't know, I responded curtly, adding that I now wished to continue my walk in peace. Courteous as ever, he withdrew, and yet again, I thought that settled things and I had escaped.

But Mr. Hughes had become my fate. He appeared in the hotel foyer that evening, greeted me simply, and we exchanged pleasantries about the weather before he slipped behind a pillar and produced an array of boxes, tins, and cases, and I found myself surrounded by a luxuriant exhibit of Indian butterflies. Spectators approached the table, Victor Hughes presented sundry British, American, and German letters of appreciation and order forms, and the larger the audience grew, the less I wanted my wretched English to be put on display. I rose abruptly, as though something important had occurred to me, left my hat and coat, and hurried to the elevator, which whisked me up to the fourth floor. In fleeing, I had handed over the reins for good.

From then on, all I saw in Kandy was my Mr. Hughes. He stood on every street corner I passed, picked up my coat when it slipped from my conveyance; he knew my room number at the hotel and what time I took my walks and meals. On the mornings I tarried until eight, I would find him by the stairs, and on days I left by six thirty, there he would be, waiting. I might be enjoying a short break in a shop, perusing the picture postcards, when suddenly he would materialize at the door with a smile and a small box under his arm, and no sooner had I swung my net in the woods and missed, than he would appear round the bend, point at the unscathed butterfly, and intone its Latin name. "I have several fine specimens of the sort, including females. I will bring them to the hotel at seven!"

Within days, he saw to it that I had nothing civil left to say, but would simply buy his wares for ten rupees. I had also earned the right to ignore him, snap at him, repel him, but he was always there, always handsome and polite with sad eyes. He addressed me warmly and lowered his slender hands in acquiescence when I berated him, and, whether early or late in the day, he always had a little box, case, or container tucked in his pocket or loincloth, always something new: first an enormous Atlas moth, then a walking leaf, rose chafer, or scorpion. He would emerge from the shadow of a pillar as I left the dining room; he was related to the merchant who sold me tooth powder and friends with the money changer I used. He found

me by the lake and at the temple, in the forest and on the street; he greeted me early in the morning after I had bathed, and he loitered, tired and disapproving, in the vestibule late at night when I left the billiards room, his head lowered politely, his eyes quiet and expectant, some treasure or other concealed in his garments. I became adept at recognizing him from afar on a crowded street and fleeing, at sensing his sudden approach and hardening my gaze; I learned to scan every branching path for his form, and to sneak from my hotel as though skipping out on a bill. He appeared repeatedly in my dreams, and it would not have surprised me to find him hiding under my bed . . .

I cannot look back on that time in Kandy without seeing him. His image is more defined than any memory of palm trees or bamboo, temples or elephants. Long after I had departed Ceylon and traveled many days by water, from time to time it would still happen: as I left my cabin for the deck in the morning, a sense of apprehension and chagrin descended and I looked over both shoulders, lest Victor Hughes should be there at the door, behind a pillar, or in the corridor, waiting for me . . .

THE BUTTERFLY

Your silver wings in flight
Over the silver heights
With red eyespots aglow
Where do you want to go?

"Out courting joy in all its breadth,
In both colorful life and death!"
—O would that God should grant
Me days as sweet and very scant!

THE PLUNDER OF SUMMER EXCURSIONS

※

One day, high summer having cooled, the painter [Hermann Lautenschlager] returned to civilization from his time away, his face sunburned and clothing soiled. He ambled cheerfully down Salzgasse and crossed the marketplace, came home to an equally dusty and disheveled apartment and unpacked, taking especial care with the big metal botanical boxes. . . .

These tins contained the plunder, skewered on fine pins, of his estival peregrinations, a couple dozen new butterflies and beetles, and Lautenschlager carefully withdrew one after another by the pin, turned and studied each, then put it aside for further work. A childlike joy and merry youthfulness flashed in his keen painter's eyes, something scarcely to be expected from this solitary, often malicious fellow, and the quiet brilliance of kindness and gratitude washed across his gaunt, sour face like the rising sun.

As is any true artist's wont, whatever his medium, Lautenschlager had maintained a path through the underbrush of an unsatisfying and unsteady life, a path back to the land of childhood that he could take whenever he wanted, where for him, as for everyone, the effulgence of dawn and the source of all powers lay hidden, a land to which he returned with a sense of utter devotion. It was the enchanting luster of fresh butterfly wings and blazing gold beetles that turned the keys of memory and opened the gates of paradise for him, a colorful sight that restored to his eyes the newness and thankful receptivity of youth for hours on end.

He gingerly carried his treasure into a small adjoining room, where two large cabinets housed his insect collection and the desk was crowded with spreading boards, packets of pins, pincushions, strips of paper, tweezers, scissors, vials of benzene, minute pliers, and other tools the well-accoutred insect collector prefers. He deposited the beetles in the appropriate cases straightaway, but spread the butterflies on the boards with great patience. Once opened, the wondrous wings looked up at him, woolly brown and gray ones, the colors matte and powdery, silvery-white ones with crystalline veins, and motley ones with a metallic enamel sheen. In his eyes, these butterfly wings were the most beautiful sight one could behold, the way other observant souls might favor flowers or mosses or the colors of the sea over other visual pleasures, and for a moment, as he regarded them, he regained what had been missing for years, namely a childlike contentedness with objects found in nature, a feeling of belonging and nearness to Creation that can be found only in a love and true understanding of natural things.

—❦—

Among certain species of moths, females are far rarer than males. They reproduce like any other creature, the male fertilizing the female, which, in turn, lays eggs. If you have one of these female moths—and many naturalists have tried this—at night the males will fly for hours to reach her! Imagine, for hours! From miles away, all these males sense the presence of the lone female in the area! Try as one might, there's no explaining it. It must be their sense of smell or something, the way good hunting dogs can pick up and track an imperceptible scent. Do you see? Nature is full of things no one can explain. But I will say this: if females were as common as males among these moths, they certainly wouldn't have such fine noses! They only have them because they've trained themselves to. When an animal or human focuses all their attention and all their resolve on one particular thing, they are bound to achieve it.

BUTTERFLIES IN LATE SUMMER

✽

The time of butterflies has come at last,
Through phlox-filled air they gently sail.
Emerging in silence from skies so vast,
Red admirals, tortoiseshells, bold swallowtails,
Silver-washed fritillaries and pale-bordered, too,
Hummingbird hawk-moth and tiger moths shy,
Mourning cloaks and painted ladies, rusty in hue.
Draped in fine furs, colors and velvet,
With a glint of jewels they float on by,
Splendid and silent, dazed and downcast,
Denizens of a fairy realm past,
Strangers here, still honeydew-wet,
From paradisial, arcadian green,
Ephemeral guests from the lands to the east,
A home long lost now seen in dreams,
Whose ghostly tidings we esteem

As a token of nobler being.
Beauty and impermanence found in the sight
Of these creatures, exalted and all too slight,
Gold-bedecked and wistful guests
Alight at the Summer King's fest!

A BUTTERFLY FROM MADAGASCAR*

⚜

But there was one thing, one gift that captured the spirit of the holiday. It was exceptional, truly spellbinding, an object one could retrieve in quiet moments and admire, a piece one could fall for, even fall in love with. I took it out and sat down by the window. Handsomely mounted under glass was a magnificent exotic butterfly that bore the lovely appellation *Urania* and had flown in from Madagascar. The beautifully built creature, with its slender, powerful swallowtail form and bold serrated hind wings, perched on a twig; its body was striped green and black on top and covered underneath in rust-colored hair, its little head a burnished golden green. The forewings were also festooned in green and black, and while the front side flaunted

---

* The species described here was once placed in the genus *Urania* but is now known as *Chrysiridia rhipheus*, the Madagascan sunset moth. The choice of the genus Urania was due to a mismatched specimen.—Translator.

a warm, ostentatious green with glints of gold, the underside displayed a cool, gentle shade of silver-kissed Veronese green, in which crystalline ribs shimmered richly. The fancifully jagged hind wings, however, featured a radiant field of gold in addition to the green-and-black pattern, a deep gold that took on a copper or even scarlet tone in the light, with whimsical flecks of black, and at the very bottom, each wing was trimmed in fine, short blond and black fur, like the hem of a lady's gown. There was another special detail: a short, dreamy line of pure white zigzagged along the edge, which essentially dissolved the wing into a haphazard play of air and gold dust and shot those fantastical tines outward like beams. At all the Christmas gatherings in the city, there was nothing more majestic, enigmatic, or alluring to be found than this butterfly from Madagascar, this airy African dream in green, black, and gold. It was a joy to return to it, a celebration to lose oneself in beholding it.

For a long time I sat hunched over the stranger from Madagascar, utterly in its thrall. It conjured up many memories, reminded me of many things, told me many tales. It was a metaphor for beauty, a metaphor for happiness, a metaphor for art. Its form was a victory over death, the play of colors a smile of superiority over evanescence. It was a multivalent smile, this dead butterfly mounted under glass, a singular smile that appeared at times childlike, at times ancient and wise, at times bellicose, at times painfully derisive—this is the smile of beauty, the smile of those forms in which life has seemingly become a thing of permanence, in which the beauty of perpetual flow has assumed shape, whether as a flower or an animal, an Egyptian bust or a death mask of a genius. It was superior and eternal, this smile, though if one looked at it for too long, it turned suddenly wild and eerie; it was beautiful and ghastly, serene and dangerous, brimming with reason and rabidity. Wherever life might appear cohesive or complete, such contradictions will emerge. Fine music will peal like children's laughter on one occasion, then on others bear down like the blackest grief. Such is beauty, and always has been: loveliness reflected in a mirror that conceals the chaos behind it. Such is happiness, and always has been: a rapturous moment that begins to fade even as it ignites, caught on the breeze of mortality. Such is high art, the high wisdom of a chosen few, and always has been: a knowing smile at the abyss, a nod to suffering, playing at harmony even as the contradictions are locked in an eternal death match.

Fleeting crimson peeked sweetly from the golden gleam, while steady black-green markings stretched taut over the ribs and the variegated points took playful aim with their darts of light. Oh, fair guest, enchanting stranger! Did you fly here from Madagascar, just to fill a winter's eve with dreams of color? Did you steal away from the eternal mother's great box of paints, just to serenade me with the wise old song about the oneness of opposites, to reteach me things I have known and so often forgotten? Did a patient human hand so ably preserve you and affix you to your twig, just to charm an ailing fellow with your dazzling antics for one lonesome hour, to console him with your silent dreams? Were you killed and pressed under glass, so that we might find solace in your immortalized suffering and death, just as we find the immortalized suffering and death of great endurers, real artists, strangely wonderful and comforting, rather than it hollowing out our soul with desperation?

Wan evening light slips across the shimmering wings, the reddish gold slowly fades, and soon the magic, swallowed by darkness, vanishes from sight. Its game with eternity continues, though, the valiant artist's bid for the permanence of beauty—in my soul the song plays on; in my mind the colors still flash gaily. The poor, beautiful butterfly from Madagascar did not die in vain, nor did that fearful hand act in vain as it preserved for posterity its wings and feelers and velvet fur. This embalmed little pharaoh will tell me stories from his sunny realm for years to come, and after he has long since decayed, and after even I have long since decayed, his blessed presence and sage smile will remain, blossom in someone else's soul and be passed on, just as Tutankhamen's gold still gleams and the blood of our Savior still flows.

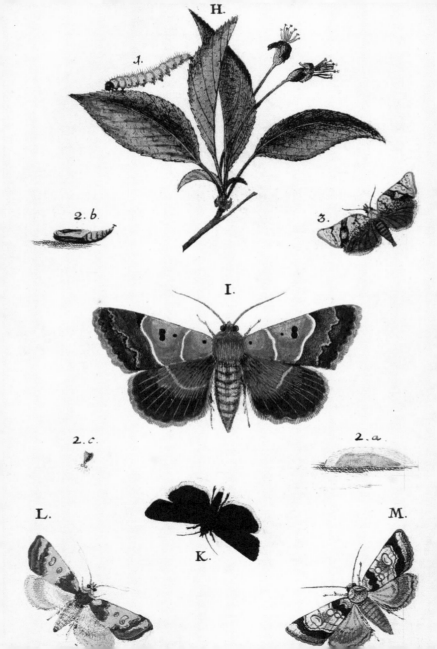

H.

1.

2.b.

3.

I.

2.c.

2.a.

L.

K.

M.

A MOTH

I return to the room, and when I turn on the light, a mighty shadow sails across the walls, and a great moth rustles quietly, hovering against the green glass globe around the light. It lands there, brightly lit, and closes its long, narrow wings, its finely feathered feelers trembling and tiny black eyes gleaming like damp beads of pitch. Fine veins branch out like marble across its folded wings, matte, broken, muted colors at play, every last brown and gray, every shade of dead leaves, soft as velvet, found in its markings. If I were Japanese, I would have inherited a trove of exact terms for these colors and their combinations and could name them. Not even that would amount to much, though, just as drawing and painting, ruminating and writing don't amount to much. The auburn, violet, and gray fields of color on these wings express the very secret of creation, all its magic, all its curses. This secret looks at us with a thousand faces, looks up, then goes out, and we cannot hold tight to any of it.

Enchantment and beauty are, alas,
Little more than hints or highs,
Such delights we know must pass,
However well they satisfy.
Flowers, bubbles, heavenly haze,
Fireworks or children's laughter,
The reflection of a woman's gaze,
All these wondrous things that, after
Arising, only last a moment,
Barely here, soon to depart,
Not but a breeze or familiar scent,
This we know with heavy heart.
The perennial is less dear to hold,
And permanence fails to inspire,
Gemstones glowing with cool fire,
Gleaming heavy bars of gold;

Even the infinite stars on high—
So unlike us mortal creatures—
Are foreign, far, cannot reach our
Souls, the depths inside.
No, the greatest beauty to be found
Is that inclined to decay,
Death itself undelayed,
And then, that most precious thing: the sound
Of music that, no sooner played,
Hastens hence, dies away,
Strains cloaked in silent grief,
Not but currents, wind, a chase,
For they can't be held in place
Past one beating of the heart;
Note after note, resonance brief,
Swiftly stream from the start.
Our hearts are loyal to all that flees,
To life and all that flows,
A brotherly sense we do not show
To solidity or guarantees.
We tire soon of steady displays,
Cliffs, jewels, and starry skies,
We, e'er adrift on our ways,

Soap-bubble souls and windy highs,
Neverlasting, wed to time,
We see dew on the rose leaf shine,
Hear birds courting, strident, gay,
Watch riven clouds fade away,
A flicker of snow, rainbows bright,
Butterflies taken off in flight,
Or we catch a mirthful peal
That glances off us in the end,
But means the world or makes us feel
Real pain. We love what is akin to us and
Are equipped to comprehend
Just what the wind has writ in sand.

THE MOURNING CLOAK

⚜

Climbing one of the granite posts on my terrace is a tall rose-bush, this year's blossoms well past, at its feet a small, lush tangle of coppertips and martagon lilies, which have slowed with age and should start blooming in a week or so. In the dazzling light, I detected something dark rising, silent and shadowy, from the verdure. It wasn't a bird but a butterfly, and none other than the mourning cloak, which has grown rare in these parts, and I had not sighted one in probably three, four years. It was a big, beautiful creature only recently hatched. Its dark form fluttered about my eyes, drifted away and back again, circled and got the measure of me before alighting on my left hand. The butterfly stayed there, closed its wings, whose sooty, ashen undersides are so dreary, then opened them again, displaying a plush violet-brown ringed in Naples yellow with a row of delightful blue dots that discreetly demarcated the bright edges from a darkness only *caput mortuum* could replicate. Slowly, to the rhythm of its calm breath, the beauty closed and opened its velvet wings, clung to the back of my hand with six capillary legs; then, after a spell and without my feeling it release, it floated away into the great, blazing brightness.

MARCH SUN

Tumbling yellow butterfly
Drunk on vernal glow.
Old man, resting hunched, just shy
Of sleep, by his window.

He too once struck out on his own,
Singing as he strode
Through springtime leaves, on wind blown
He passed o'er dusty roads.

While these butterflies golden
And blossoming boughs
Appear barely oldened,
Appeared then as now.

But colors and smells have, it's fair,
Grown thinner now, more barren.
The light is cooler and the air
Is hard to breathe, so leaden.

Springtime, soft as bees in flight,
Hums songs true and sweet.
Heavens sway, blue and white,
The butterfly in gold retreat.

LATE SUMMER

A late-summer gift, day after day
Of sweet warmth. Umbels below,
The butterfly drifts along its way,
Tired wings a golden glow.

Evening and morning expire damp breath,
Thin fog, a balmy brume.
When from the mulberry tree a flash,
Yellow leaf adrift in the gloom.

Grapes hide away in the green,
While lizards bask on warmed stone.
The world seems enchanted, asleep, in a dream
And warns you to leave it alone.

Music, too, will often dwell
In eternity incandescent,
Then, waking, wrests us from the spell
Back to courage and the present.

We, the aged, are harvesting here,
Warming our summer-kissed fingers.
The day not yet over, the sun still lingers
And flatters and holds us near.

Since time immemorial, butterflies have captured the imagina-
tion of people from all walks of life, among them artists, phi-
losophers, and scientists. Paintings of butterflies decorated the
walls of pharaohs' tombs as far back as 1500 B.C.E., and gold
jewelry crafted in their likeness was found in the crypts of My-
cenaean princes from 1300 B.C.E. Even the Buddha (560–480
B.C.E.) is said to have addressed his final sermon to butterflies:
"I have learned more from you than from all the writings of the
Brahmans." Ancient Greeks viewed butterflies as both a man-
ifestation of the soul and a symbol of its immortality; moths
within the family known today as Psychidae were worshipped
in pre-Christian Greece as the souls of the departed. Aristo-
tle (384–322 B.C.E.) was the first to describe the lepidopteran
metamorphosis from egg to caterpillar to pupa to winged insect. Then a cultural shift occurred, and butterflies no longer

represented death and rebirth, but became a symbol of grace and love associated with Eros and Aphrodite as well as Psyche.

Our knowledge of butterflies and moths has grown steadily since then. Starting with clunky fossils from the Permian period, over 270 million years ago, we have charted their evolution into more than 177,000 known species. They live all around the world, from Greenland to the southernmost tip of South America, a diversity that can be attributed to their extraordinary adaptability. (Butterflies and moths can be found in the Arctic tundra, scorching deserts, and tropical rain forests. The eggs of several species can withstand temperatures from −80 to 130 degrees Fahrenheit.)

Over the centuries, entomologists steadily expanded their butterfly charts. Classification systems—which group biological organisms by genus, family, and other taxonomic ranks—were introduced, and illustrations became more precise: the rudimentary outline of wings captured in woodcuts gave way to the loving exactitude of copperplate engravings, while the realism of photography later yielded to the resolution of electron microscopes.

Ours is no longer an ignorant delight in admiring the brilliance and range of butterfly ornamentation. The dream of beauty for beauty's sake is now countered by an understanding of reason and function. With the help of a microscope, we discovered a mosaic created by the hundreds of thousands of tiny scales that cover the wings' transparent membrane like roof tiles. We know that only yellows, reds, browns, and blacks are produced by pigments, whereas nearly all other hues are interference colors created when light hits the scales and diffracts. While many of these are ultraviolet and indistinguishable to humans, insects perceive a far more extensive and intense spectrum with their compound eyes. We no longer puzzle over the remarkable fact that a butterfly's luster can last for decades after its death: color is stored in the chitinous wing scales, thus protecting it from organic decay. Studies have shown that by the pupa stage, skin cells in the wings have concentrated their pigments in the lifeless part of the scales. The display of color often depends on the temperature, too. Eyespots, for instance, commonly emerge when temperatures climb and the rainy season begins, whereas cooler weather brings out camouflage patterns.

Butterflies' prodigal apparel helps them identify and attract mates and protects them by drawing predators' attention away from their vulnerable bodies. After all, butterflies and moths represent the final stage of existence, the sole purpose of which is reproduction; this period is very brief, considering the lengthy metamorphosis preceding it.

The immobile, nondescript eggs are "incubated" by the sun and hatch into ravenous, ungainly larvae. Caterpillars are not particularly alluring; nor do they need to be, as mating is not of concern. They focus instead on eating and fending off predators before reverting to a state of outward stillness and armored inconspicuousness as a pupa. Then comes the butterfly: weightless, agile, and more fetching than at any stage of its youth, which it happily survived. While as larvae they devour certain plants by the hundredweight, and accommodate the consequences of such vegetative, infantile consumption by shedding their skin repeatedly, some butterflies survive entirely without food: winged energy devoted to reproduction and pollination. Of course most butterflies and moths do require additional sustenance. They use their coiled proboscis, which resembles a clock spring and extends to double the length of the body in some species, to feed from blossoms, trees, fruit, and even animal matter (both feces and rotting carcasses), though this diet amounts to a mere fraction of what fueled their development.

A natural corollary to butterflies' survival instinct is the role they play in helping host plants multiply. Like most winged insects, they contribute to the greater ecological picture as pollinators. Attracted by color and fragrance, butterflies carry pollen picked up from a flower's (male) stamen to the (female) pistil, thus securing a food source for their own offspring by ensuring that the plants will grow again next season. Butterflies can perceive differences in color, pattern, and smell as nuanced as their own features. In other words, a butterfly is as sensitive to its environment as it is charismatic. The same goes for its ability to send and receive high-frequency, ultrasonic signals.

Unlike most other insects, butterflies actually appear related to flowers. Not only is the delicate consistency of their wings reminiscent of petals; their size and color also correspond to the flora around them, which explains why tropical butterflies are bigger and brighter than those in temperate zones. (Their wing spans range from a few millimeters, as seen in the midget moth, to nearly twelve inches among some equatorial lepidopterans.)

Flower petals emerge from the bud in much the same way a butterfly unfolds its papery wings from along its welt-like body after it has hatched from the cocoon, wings that may quintuple in size. Harbingers of spring, both butterflies and flowers are associated with nature's regeneration after a cold, dark winter. And yet another similarity between the two: just as blossoms open with the sun and close as it sets, after a chilly night butterflies will stretch their wings toward the light and the invigorating warmth of the sun. Whether of petals or wings, it's the sunny side that's intended to allure, whereas the markings below are so nondescript as to suggest a different species entirely. After all, the undersides are meant not to entice, but to camouflage and protect. Butterflies and moths sleep—and a few species even hibernate—in this comparatively dull state.

The great diversity and splendor of their colors and patterns, fine and ephemeral as flowers, though untethered and free in weightless flight between heaven and earth, have long inspired artists to create. Poets have called butterflies "winged flowers" and shown them the attention and preference characteristic of elective affinities. In a world that values performance-driven usefulness and a settled way of life, artists have always been admired, envied, and mistrusted as outsiders, their independence interpreted as flightiness or their sense of beauty construed as elitist and irresponsible. Artists and butterflies are simpatico, the shared nature of their existence explored by writers from Zhuangzi to Catullus, Eduard Mörike to Hans Christian Andersen. Tellingly, Andersen's butterfly—a fickle and inveterate bachelor at odds with the rooted, staid world of women— meets his end in a bourgeois sitting room. There the butterfly, now pinned in place beside a houseplant, muses, "Here I am, stuck to a stalk like a flower. It is not pleasant, though this must be what marriage is like: you're stuck."

The German poet Hellmut von Cube wrote about the utility of this seemingly asocial insect in his *Tierskizzenbüchlein* (Little Book of Animal Sketches):

Bees buzz industriously, ants scurry and haul, . . . beetles scrabble about importantly, worms dig and hollow out with great purpose, but the butterfly has nothing planned. It swings and dances here and there, sips nectar, bobbing as it rests, then lets the gentle wind carry it aloft, only to drop back down with a soft, playful beat of its wings, like the air, like a trice, like God's will. . . . The hedgehog eats mice and adders: a respectable lad; the cow is useful from horns to hoofs, milk to manure: what a decent animal! The butterfly, meanwhile, flies from blossom to blossom, yet produces no honey, that ne'er-do-well.

The earth is mighty, heavy and massive with its mountains, its elephants, iron and lead. . . . It would be unendurable without butterflies, without the little umbrellas of dandelion blossoms. . . . A single butterfly lessens the weight of the world; all heaviness, all matter is rendered null at the sight.

Among twentieth-century German writers, surely none was drawn to butterflies like Hermann Hesse. Butterflies appear as symbols for the transience of beauty as well as incremental change in all his writings, from stories and novels to reflections and poems, and even in pieces whose titles would not suggest their presence (as in several works in this volume). "I have always had an affinity to butterflies and other ephemeral beauties," Hesse wrote in a letter dated January 1926, "whereas I have never had much success with lasting or 'solid' relationships." (He said this in reference to his first two marriages, while the opposite was true for his friendships.)

One of Hesse's earliest memories dates back to when he was five. He and his parents were living at 26 Müllerweg in Basel, "across from Spalenring. . . . [It was] a rather modest neighborhood just outside the city, though for us children it was paradise, a jungle of endless discovery and adventure. Not far from the house, it turned into countryside . . . and the Schützenmatte, a vast expanse for a small child, where the shooting club had not yet been built and the park extended all the way to 'Neubad,' served as my butterfly hunting grounds."

In his first autobiographical book, *Hermann Lauscher*, which he wrote at age nineteen, Hesse describes the "breathless, heart-pounding elation" he felt as a five-year-old admiring these creatures of the air, "along with the peculiar conviction that that time and that meadow alone could produce such wonderful quaking grasses and butterflies. . . . On certain bright mornings I would stretch out in the grass, head on my hands, and gaze over the crinkled sea of grasses glimmering in the sunlight." It was the first time he could escape the "world of separation" and enter a "world of unity, where one thing or creature says to the other: *Tat tvam asi* ('That thou art')." The novelty of the experience made a lasting impression. The meadow and its butterflies became lifelong archetypes, inextinguishable engrams, "fleeting metaphors" of "immortal things."

Pen-and-ink illustration by Gunter Böhmer, from
Hesse's autobiographical *Hermann Lauscher*.

That little boy's ingenuous and selfless fascination with butterflies gave way to the nine- or ten-year-old's impulse to catch them, the "nameless, hungry delight that only children feel," though he showed minimal regard for his spoils and never assembled a proper collection. From the ages of nine to twelve—if "The Giant Peacock Moth" is any indication—his love of the sport first peaked. Young Hesse became so obsessed that his parents considered forbidding the hobby, as their son was forgetting or neglecting his other obligations. "While out chasing butterflies, I was deaf to the clock tower sounding the start of school or lunchtime, and during vacations I'd often set out in the early morning and not return till night, not come home for a single meal, with just a bit of bread packed in my botanical box." This passion was as fiery as its end.

"Of all the butterflies and moths I could name that were missing from my box, there were none I coveted as desperately [as the giant peacock moth]," Hesse writes in retrospect, in the voice of the character Heinrich Mohr. Naturally it would be the least likable boy in the neighborhood to net this rare creature. The young protagonist of the story is desperate to see the treasure, a curiosity so intense it eclipses inhibition and leads him to steal for the first time. To his own astonishment and horror, he realizes what he is doing before the deed is even done. In his fear of being caught, he ends up damaging the specimen. He is more troubled by the sight of the destroyed moth than he is by the fact of having stolen, such that "I would have given anything, any possession, any pleasure, to have it restored." He eventually confesses to his pedantic classmate, whose primary "vice" is that of "flawlessness" and whom the narrator detests "out of equal parts envy and admiration." He offers him all his toys, then his entire butterfly collection, but the attempt at expiation fails. He returns home and destroys his beloved butterflies, one by one, enraged by his schoolmate's arrogant contempt and disturbed by how easily his excitement got the better of him.

A newly unearthed eyewitness account reveals a great deal about the relationship between fact and fiction in Hesse's quasi-autobiographical stories. In a letter from May 31, 1952, addressed to Alfred Leuschner, secretary of the Basel Mission, the eighty-year-old Pastor Benedikt Hartmann shared his memories of Hermann Hesse, who was four years his junior and with whom he had attended the Basel Mission School from 1884 to 1886. The sturdy youngster, who spoke "Swabian-inflected High German," didn't make much of an impression: "The other boys and I only became aware of him following an occurrence that caused quite a stir and devastated his reputation."

One of their teachers—a great stenographer, a green thumb, a philatelist, and an accomplished butterfly collector—owned an "unusually large and magnificently colored moth." One day, the meticulously preserved and mounted specimen vanished "from the teacher's room, which was situated between two classrooms and left unlocked. The culprit turned out to be Hermann Hesse, whose enthusiasm for this natural artwork was shot through with notions of possession. I don't believe an exemplary punishment was meted out, though there was scarcely a need for it among a pack of boarding school boys, and he returned to it himself as a writer, like Saint Augustine in his *Confessions*."

In the fictionalized version of events, recounted by a first-person narrator's houseguest, the author directs the reader's sympathies toward the perpetrator of the theft, rather than its victim. There is a good chance that Hesse's teacher humiliated him with the same withering words he put in the mouth of the Perfect Boy.

This experience put an end to Hesse's love of collecting for years to come. When, at age twenty-eight, he unwittingly lands in Preda during a hiking trip in Graubünden, his defenses remain intact, and he observes the humor of the mania surrounding the Alpine tiger moth objectively, with an irony gained through having survived a past obsession.

There in Preda, Hesse stumbles upon a cadre of eccentric vacationers who call themselves entomologists, which he soon learns is the academic name for butterfly and insect collectors. "I always thought catching butterflies was for children," he remarks in astonishment. The response he receives reveals much about the psychology of adult collectors: "If you aren't an entomologist, what brings you to Preda?" It would never occur to these men that the town might have its own appeal, from its stunning location amid Alpine meadows at six thousand feet above sea level to its forests and magnificent terrain. They are collectors, people whose blind sense of purpose is all the more amplified, the more limited their range of perception and specialized their interests. After his childhood experience with the giant peacock moth, Hesse is ready for the men's vagaries and has his attention trained on their behavior:

There are those among them, no doubt, who would prove pleasant in everyday life, but here on the playground of their passions, they become fanatical and impossible. . . . Each keeps a close eye on the others. After making a rare catch, a fellow will fib about where he

found it, unaware that at least one of his comrades was trailing
him and noted the site. . . . And should a dreaded rival topple over
a wall and break his bones, the others receive the news with poorly
feigned sympathy.

A few years after this episode in the Alps with his friends
Emanuel von Bodman and Ludwig Finckh, Hesse's children
took to collecting butterflies and discovered an old hand in
their father, who was overcome by a past enthusiasm he had
thought irretrievable. Hesse's sons recall expeditions they took
to fields around Lake Constance and woodlands near Bern. In
his 1953 reflection "Hermann Hesse and Butterflies," one of
Hesse's writer friends, Wilhelm Schussen, describes an experience the men shared in Gaienhofen:

I recall that we were discussing plants and butterflies, that I
pointed out the great burnet (Sanguisorba officinalis) growing
there, and that Hesse revealed himself to be a canny authority
on the subject of butterflies. . . . This indescribable fellow abruptly
charged toward a hedge and flapped his arms like wings, send-
ing a swarm of ginger-colored butterflies into the air. His gaunt
face, with its pointy chin and even pointier nose, was thoroughly
birdlike in that moment, while the rest of him, down to his knee

breeches, calves, and sandals, appeared enraptured, distant, otherworldly. And it looked like the hedge had caught fire as this cloud of orange butterflies swirled around his head. "That's the small tortoiseshell," Hesse said after a while, as though returning from someplace else. . . . Wherever he may tarry, in my mind's eye he will forever remain by that burning bush." (From *Hermann Hesse in Augenzeugenberichten*, [Frankfurt: Suhrkamp, 1987/1991]

That period saw an old love rekindled for the thirty-year-old. Hesse created his first proper collection, which grew considerably following a three-month trip to Indonesia, from September to December 1911. His travel diary, which reads like shorthand, documents at least fifty-five hours spent stalking exotic butterflies on the Malay Peninsula, in Sumatra, and in Sri Lanka, then under British colonial rule and known as Ceylon. In an entry composed after visiting a museum in Singapore, Hesse simply lists the butterflies on display there. His notebook mentions the importunate butterfly dealer Victor Hughes by name and details the Malays' amusement at the sight of this weird European with his big net. A further parallel to the story "Indian Butterflies" appears in a missive from Hesse to the Swiss painter Max Bucherer, a friend and fellow entomology enthusiast. In this letter, much as he did to ward off the pushy insect peddler in Kandy, Hesse stresses his preference for fresh specimens that have not yet been preserved. Two months after his return from India, he wrote to Bucherer:

I would be delighted to accept any butterflies or beetles you wish to give me. I could especially use those that are not yet preserved, happy to do it myself. In exchange, the next time you see my collection, you'll have to pick out some doubles of the Indian butterflies I caught. It's not a great many, though there certainly are some nice ones. In total I brought home about 300 butterflies and moths, many in duplicate or triplicate.

In the third and fourth decades of his life, Hesse's interest in butterflies—a fascination he shared, incidentally, with his Russian American contemporary Vladimir Nabokov (1899–1977)—pivoted away from pragmatism and toward an appreciation of their diversity. But as his sons grew and the First World War began, this phase waned, and for the rest of his life, Hesse's love of butterflies occupied a more contemplative space. The appeal of these later depictions—of the butterfly from Madagascar, the mottled moth in "A Moth," and the mourning cloak in Hesse's diary from 1955—no longer derives from the adventurous exploits of youth. Freed of the compulsion to portray the creatures, he instead delights in their manifestations of life. The precision of his appreciation rouses associations and analogies that illuminate the big picture in the details, the symbolism in the likeness. A butterfly in flight now suggests:

a victory over death, the play of colors a smile of superiority over evanescence. . . . This is . . . the smile of those forms in which life has seemingly become a thing of permanence, in which the beauty of perpetual flow has assumed shape. . . . A rapturous moment that begins to fade even as it ignites . . . playing at harmony even as the contradictions are locked in an eternal death match.

Hesse's letter to his sister Adele in late 1913 reads like a goodbye: "Catching butterflies and fishing were my two great pleasures in life, nothing else particularly dear to me." A later communication reveals his increasing reluctance to kill animals:

I caught butterflies and fish in my younger years, but stopped when my reservations about killing outweighed the drive to hunt. . . . One who bags game blindly is a bad hunter. A good hunter is one who exercises moderation in shooting and takes equal care in tending game as he does in ending its life. Similarly, a butterfly collector . . . can do things here and there to counter the extinction of certain species and their host plants; this is all he can offer nature to compensate for what he steals from it.

For that very reason, at his homes on Lake Constance, in Bern, or in Ticino, Hesse's gardens included patches of stinging nettles, a primary food source for butterfly larvae.

We don't need to be entomologists to see, in the bleak global extinction rates of flora and fauna, just how advanced the destruction of our biosphere is. Three-quarters of the approximately four thousand butterfly and moth species native to Germany have already vanished over the past twenty-five years. Our myopic approach to modern agriculture seeks only to exploit and threatens to disrupt the natural equilibrium in many areas, as countless small animal species and microorganisms have fallen victim to land consolidation, monocultures, biochemical fertilizers, and the large-scale use of chemical insecticides. What is technologically feasible is rapidly outpacing our ability to harness it in a way that ensures that benefits extend beyond the current moment. Industrial, chemical, and nuclear developments in recent decades have wreaked such damage on the environment that the preservation of land, air, water, and food sources has become the stuff of political platforms.

Butterflies are an essential part of the natural world, connected in myriad ways to the plants and animals around them. They pollinate flowers and serve as food for little creatures like ants, frogs, lizards, and birds. Their larvae produce stunning amounts of excrement, which helps regenerate soil. The drastic decline in butterfly populations should serve as a warning sign to industrial nations whose prosperity comes at the cost of a natural world out of balance.

A world in which the ostensibly useless butterfly can flourish is the only one worthy of human life and love.

Volker Michels

⟶⟵

Hermann Hesse wrote the opening essay, "About Butterflies," in 1935 as a preface to Adolf Portmann's book of photography *Falterschönheit* (Butterfly Beauty), released in 1936. The prose passages in this volume follow the biographical events described, a chronology not necessarily reflected in the respective publication dates. The poems, meanwhile, are intended to highlight thematic aspects and are placed accordingly.

To illustrate this collection, we sought out old, hand-colored copperplate engravings, which, Hesse argued, "were far more lovely and, indeed, far more precise than any modern color prints." In a letter to Hans Popp in 1943, he wrote:

As for flowers, butterflies, etc., the heyday of artistic rendering fell sometime between 1750 and 1800, when drawings were engraved in copper and colored by hand, and not only are these images prettier and more appealing than the best technical reproductions, they're also more accurate. It's easier to identify plants, beetles, etc., in copperplates from that time than in today's best illustrations.

Thus, the engravings included in this collection were originally made by the entomologist, painter, and textiles designer Jakob Hübner (1761–1826) of Augsburg. They were reproduced from *Beiträge zur Geschichte der Schmetterlinge* (Contributions to the History of Butterflies, 1786–1790), *Das kleine Schmetterlingsbuch* (The Little Butterfly Book, 1934), *Hübner's Papilio* (Hübner's Butterflies, 1796–1841), and *Sammlung exotischer Schmetterlinge* (Collection of Exotic Butterflies, 1806).

SOURCES

The following dates of writing and publication, and the location of the original texts in Hesse's Complete Works (*Sämtliche Werke*, ed. Volker Michels, 20 vols. [Frankfurt: Suhrkamp, 2001–07], citations by volume and page number), are taken from the German edition of *Butterflies*, with places of first publication and details about revisions and newspaper editions versus book publication omitted. Titles followed by an asterisk were supplied by the German-language editor, Volker Michels, for untitled poems or excerpts from longer works.

"On Butterflies": Written 1935. XIV:172.

"A Butterfly"*: Written September 1904. X:199.

"My Earliest Memory"*: Written 1896. First published November 1900. From *Hermann Lauscher*. I:226.

"Blue Butterfly": Written December 1927. X:307.

"The Giant Emperor Moth": Written 1911. VIII:14.

"Dedication to a Poetry Collection": Written May 27, 1934. X:326.

"Apollo: A Day's Wanderings About Lake Lucerne": Written 1901. I:493.

"Butterfly in Wine": Written July 6, 1919. X:261.

"The Yellow Tiger Moth": Written 1905. XIII:97.

"Confession": Written January 21, 1918. X:246.

"Indian Butterflies": Written 1912. XIII:263.

"The Butterfly": Written 1902. X:516.

"The Plunder of Summer Excursions"*: Written 1917. From "In a Small City." VI:575.

"From *Demian*": Written 1917. First published November 1919. From *Demian*. III:276.

"Butterflies in Late Summer": Written 1933. X:322.

"A Butterfly from Madagascar"*: Written 1928. From "After Christmas." XIV:58.

"A Moth"*: Written 1930. From "Between Summer and Autumn." XIV:159.

"Writ in Sand": Written September 16–17, 1947. X:379.

"The Mourning Cloak"*: Written 1955. From "Diary Entries." XI:740.

"March Sun": Written March 14, 1948. X:381.

"Late Summer": Written September 23, 1940. X:364.

The following species' historical Latin names are taken from the Biodiversity Heritage Library's original German editions of Jakob Hübner's works:

- *Beiträge zur Geschichte der Schmetterlinge* (Augsburg: Der Verfasser, 1786–90; Cornell University Library); abbreviated here as BGS.

- *Das kleine Schmetterlingsbuch* (Leipzig: Insel-Verlag, 1934; Duke University Libraries); DKS.

- *Hübner's Papilio* (S.l.: s.n., 1796–1841; Cornell University Library); HP.

- *Sammlung exotischer Schmetterlinge* (Augsburg: Im Verlag der Hübner'schen Werke, 1806–41; Smithsonian Libraries); SES.

The locations of the original images in Jakob Hübner's oeuvre are cited by the abbreviations listed above (BGS, DKS, HP, SES) and their page or plate numbers. Some species have been reclassified and some have gone extinct; thus the historical names used here may be difficult to cross-reference. Common names for species have been added when known.

FRONT COVER *(from the top)* *Gonopterix rhamni*, common brimstone. DKS:13–1. | *Pieris brassicae*, large white. DKS:16–2. | *Thais polyxena*. DKS:18–1. | *Colias hyale*, pale clouded yellow. DKS:28–1. | *Papilio machaon*, Old World swallowtail. DKS:17–3.

PAGE i Phalaena Geometra bombycata. BGS:II–14K.

PAGE ii *(from top left to right)* Lycaena argus. DKS:19–2. | *Argynnis aglaia*, dark-green fritillary. DKS:9–1. | *Hamadryades Undatae odius*. SES:55. | *Phalaena Noctua umbra*, bordered sallow. BGS:II–24O. | *Arachnia prorsa*, map (summer brood). DKS:11–1. | *Potamides Conspicuae teucer*. SES:77. | *Hamadryas Decora calliroë*. SES:46.

PAGE iv *(from top left to right)* Phalaena Geometra trilinearia, clay triple-lines. BGS:II–24T. | *Principes Dominantes philenor*. SES:129. | *Bombyces Sphingoides caecigaena*. HP:72–302. | *Pararge megaera*, wall brown. DKS:13–5 | *Hamadryades Decorae evarete*. SES:51. | *Limnades Subtiles pharea*. SES:32. | *Limnades Thalassicae limniace*. SES:19.

PAGE v *(from the top)* Najades Moderatae alcithoë. SES:64. | *Phalaena Geometra sanguinaria*. BGS:II–24S.

PAGE x *Najades Hilares themis*. SES:60.

PAGE 8 *Phalaena Noctua modefta*. BGS:I–3 (A). | *Phalaena Pyralis guttalis*, white-spotted sable (B). | *Phalaena Tinea combinella* (C). | *Phalaena Tinea pufiella* (D: a, b, c, d). | *Phalaena Noctua affinis*, lesser-spotted pinion (E). | *Phalaena Noctua fulvago*, angle-striped sallow (F). | *Phalaena Noctua octogesimea*, figure of eighty (G).

PAGE 9 *Euchloe cardamines*, orange tip. DKS:22 (1, 2). | *Colias edusa*, clouded yellow (3, 4).

PAGE 12 *Callophris rubi*, green hairstreak. DKS:15 (1, 2). | *Chrysophanus virgaureae*, scarce copper (3, 4). | *Chrysophanus phlaeas*, small copper (5, 6).

PAGE 15 *Parnassius apollo*, Apollo. DKS:23 (1, 2). | *Parnassius mnemosyne*, clouded Apollo (3).

PAGE 18 *Dryades Fucatae claudia*. SES:42 (1, 2 male | 3, 4 female).

PAGE 22 *Lycaena arion*, large blue. DKS:12 (1, 2). | *Lycaena icarus*, common blue (3, 4, 5).

PAGE 24 *Vanessa jo*, European peacock. DKS:6 (1, 2). | *Vanessa antiopa*, mourning cloak (3, 4).

PAGE 29 *Apatura ilia*, lesser purple emperor. DKS:24 (1, 2). | *Apatura iris*, purple emperor (3, 4).

PAGE 36 *(from top left to right) Argynnis daphne*, marbled fritillary. DKS:8–3. | *Bombyces Verae quercus*. HP:64–270. | *Melitaea cinxia*, Glanville fritillary. DKS:10–3.

PAGE 37 *(clockwise from left to top right) Limnades Thalassicae idea*. SES:18 | *Limnades Ferrugineae plexippe*. SES:20. | *Echidnae Comuniformes tarquinius*. SES:176. | *Phalaena Geometra luctuata*. BGS:I–33Y.

PAGE 48 *Bombyces Verae hera*. HP:27–116. | *Bombyces Verae dominula*, scarlet tiger (117, 118).

PAGE 52 *Limnas Ferrugineae chrysippus*. SES:22 (1, 2 male | 3, 4 female).

PAGE 53 *Potamides Superbae thalpius*. SES:71.

PAGE 54 *(from the top) Arachnia levana*, map. DKS:11–4. | *Papilio podalirius*, scarce swallowtail. DKS:17–1. | *Bombyces Verae avia*. HP:53–230. | *Bombyces Sphingoides cecropia*, HP:67–282.

PAGE 55 *Phalaena Geometra lunularia*. BGS:III–28T.

PAGE 63 *(from the top) Phalaena Geometra liturata*, tawny-barred angle. BGS:IV–32X. | *Phalaena Geometra strigillaria*, grass wave. BGS:II–14I. | *Phalaena Alucita dodecadactyla*. BGS:I–33R. | *Phalaena Geometra sylveftrata*.

BGS:I–33S. | *Phalaena Geometra prafinaria.* BGS:IV–24S. | *Phalaena Tinea cribrumella.* BGS:I–33W. | *Phalaena Bombyces abietis.* BGS:II–3A. | *Phalaena Geometra lunaria.* BGS:IV–3C.

PAGE 66 *Satyrus hermione,* woodland grayling. DKS:21 (1, 2, 3). | *Satyrus alcyone,* rock grayling (4, 5).

PAGE 72 *Pyrameis cardui,* painted lady. DKS:7 (1, 2). | *Pyrameis atalanta,* red admiral. (3, 4).

PAGE 73 *Phalaena Noctua fafcia.* BGS:II–14H.

PAGE 74 *Lares Heroicae leilaria.* SES:200.

PAGE 80 *Phalaena Tortrix cerafana,* barred fruit-tree. BGS:I–14H (1, 2, 3). | *Phalaena Noctua lunaris* (I). | *Phalaena Pyralis marginalis,* melonworm moth (K). | *Phalaena Noctua rutilago* (L). | *Phalaena Noctua ochracea,* frosted orange moth (M).

PAGE 82 *Oreades Coruscae sapphira.* SES:96 (1, 2 male | 3, 4 female).

PAGE 85 *Polygonia c-album,* comma. DKS:10–1.

PAGE 86 *Vanessa polychloros,* large tortoiseshell. DKS:5 (1, 2). | *Vanessa urticae,* small tortoiseshell (3, 4).

PAGE 88 *Satyrus arethusa,* false grayling. DKS:20–3.

PAGE 91 *Mancipium Fugacia argante.* SES:145 (1, 2 male | 3, 4 female).

PAGE 92 *Najades Turbidae pipleis.* SES:65.

PAGE 94 *(from the top) Bombyces Verae carpini.* HP:14–54. | *Phalaena Noctua moneta,* golden plusia. BGS:III–28P. | *Phalaena Noctua diffinis,* white-spotted pinion. BGS:IV–32T. | *Echidnae Caudatae selene.* SES:174.

PAGE 95 *(clockwise from top left) Bombyces Sphingoides harpagula.* HP:11–43. | *Phalaena Bombyces lupulina.* BGS:I–33T. | *Phalaena Geometra lineolata.* BGS:II–28V. | *Phalaena Noctua purpurina.* BGS:II–14G. | *Mancipia Voracia hyparete.* SES:138. | *Argynnis paphia,* silver-washed fritillary. DKS:I–9.

PAGE 96 *(from the top)* *Phalaena Geometra fulvata.* BGS:IV–32V. | *Phalaena Noctua unita.* BGS:I–33V. | *Phalaena Geometra vernaria*, little emerald. BGS:IV–3D. | *Phalaena Geometra sexalifata.* BGS:III–22. | *Phalaena Tortrix literana*, sprinkled rough-wing. BGS:III–22. | *Phalaena Bombyces flexula.* BGS:I:33.

PAGE 103 *Lares Heroicae empedoclaria.* SES:201.

PAGE 104 *Potamides Conspicuae menelaus.* SES:81.

PAGE 118 *Potamides Conspicuae leonte.* SES:80.

PAGE 121 *Hamadryades Undatae astina.* SES:56.

PAGE 122 *Hamadryades Decorae amphinome*, red cracker. SES:47.

BACK COVER *Echidnae Comuniformes cytherea.* SES:175.

HERMANN HESSE was born in 1877 in Calw, Germany. He rose to become a celebrated author and the recipient of the Nobel Prize in Literature in 1946. As the son of missionaries, he developed a fascination with self-discovery and spiritual explorations, an interest also likely due in part to his lifelong struggle with depression, which led him to study Sigmund Freud and, later, to undergo psychoanalysis with Carl Jung. In 1912 he moved to Switzerland, where he wrote his best-known books, including the classic *Siddhartha*; composed poetry; and painted landscapes. He passed away in 1962 in Montagnola, Switzerland. Hesse is one of the most widely translated authors of the twentieth century; his work continues to have influence worldwide.

VOLKER MICHELS is primarily known for his work as an editor at the Frankfurt publishing house Suhrkamp Verlag (which later expanded to include Insel Verlag). There, his focus from 1969 to 2008 was to make the works of Hermann Hesse more accessible and to advance the Nobel laureate's literary and artistic legacy; this included editing the first complete edition of his writings, consisting of approximately fifteen thousand pages in twenty volumes. Michels is the world's foremost authority on Hesse's work and also manages his literary and artistic estate.

JAKOB HÜBNER lived from 1761 to 1826 and was an Augsburg entomologist, painter, and textiles designer acclaimed for his colorful copper engravings, known as chalcographies, illustrating insects, flowers, and other natural wonders. This technique was among Hermann Hesse's favorites, as he thought it to be much more precise and beautiful than modern reproductions. Hübner's book *Sammlung europäischer Schmetterlinge* (Collection of European Butterflies), first published at the turn of the nineteenth century, is considered to be a foundational work in entomology.

ELISABETH LAUFFER has translated more than a dozen books from German into English, with a focus on contemporary fiction and literary nonfiction. She is the recipient of numerous honors, including the Gutekunst Prize for Emerging Translators, participation in the Art Omi: Writers Translation Lab and KulturKontakt Austria Artists-in-Residence program, and, most recently, acceptance into the ViceVersa workshop at Translation House Looren in Switzerland. Her rendering of *Pollak's Arm*, by Hans von Trotha, was named to the Kirkus list of Best Fiction in Translation of 2022.